EVERYDAY
LOVE
LETTERS
for CHRISTIANS

LETTERS *for* CHRISTIANS

Tiekie PRESS

Letters for Christians series
Everyday Love Letters for Christians

Copyright © Pieter de Kock, 2024
All rights reserved.

First published 2024 by Tiekie Press

ISBN 978-1-0686586-3-1

Edited and typeset by Copy–editing Services
https://copy-editing.org/

Cover design by Pieter de Kock

EVERYDAY LOVE

for
Ilse
André

Teach us to number our days,
that we may gain a heart of wisdom
—Psalm 90:12 (NIV)

LETTERS *for* CHRISTIANS

FOREWORD

Reading these letters was like strolling through the many beautiful conversations we have had spanning 42 years; each one a glimpse into the way Pieter sees. I met Pieter in 1982 and since 1987 our friendship has been separated by thousands of miles—and yet it has grown ever closer with the passing years. In this time I have seen how Pieter chooses to see what is not always obvious—to envision a different outcome than the facts in that moment suggest. The musings recorded in this book are evidence of that and are a reminder of the divinity of every minute of our day. They have encouraged me to look for the hand of a Loving God constantly at work in my life; to incline my ears to hear His whisper as I learn to "live loved"—in the confidence of His perfect leadership in my life. As you take the time to read these letters I am sure that you too will feel the urge to pick up a pen, find some paper and start writing. I pray that it births in you a desire to communicate love in a more intentional way, as together we discover more of what it means to love one another. Pieter, thank you for the encouragement that is embodied in these letters.

Juan Swart

LETTERS *for* CHRISTIANS

EVERYDAY LOVE

PREFACE

There are numerous excellent inspirational Christian books available for almost every type of reader, the most prolific being calendar-based where messages combined with selected Bible verses are presented for every day of the year. This smaller format pocketbook containing 90 letters is different in that it's we who write to THE LORD. HE is after all our FATHER and we, HIS children. It's a book intended for readers of all ages and levels of maturity in Christ. These letters focus on the ordinary and how we might find meaning in unlikely places; but however we might want to frame our thoughts, writing letters has the potential to lead to great personal spiritual growth. Each letter ends with a short prayer to set the mind for when it's time to pick up our own Bible and explore the full context of GOD's word. Let's start writing letters and may they bear fruit for they are our own unique precious conversations with the LORD through JESUS CHRIST our Saviour.

Blessings
—may the Lord be with you always.

Amen

LETTERS *for* CHRISTIANS

EVERYDAY LOVE

INTRODUCTION

This pocketbook is a call to Christians to find joy again in the simple act of letter writing. Whether it's a letter to say goodbye, of encouragement, to say sorry, to teach, or just to share news and ideas, letters are capable of transforming the way we think. It's something we've forgotten about because of the convenience of instant communication but it's intriguing to think back on lives lived, how easy it is to understand things better from words written down on paper. It's the modest letter which somehow still manages to most exquisitely capture the meaning and emotion in a message. We know how the Bible itself is a compilation of handwritten letters; and Paul's use of letters was to inspire people to spread the good news. So, for Christians today it's useful to hold on to the tradition of letter writing while we're here, for the very short time that we're here. Let's then encourage one another with love, to restore the value of, and role played by handwritten letters in Christian faith.

Lord, encourage us to write more letters.

Amen

EVERYDAY LOVE

1
LETTER FOR YOU

Psalm 90 is the oldest of the psalms which became 'a letter' of song and prayer. Would there have been anything better than receiving a scroll of a message passed down from someone as dear as Moses? Can our lives today, as crammed as they are with email and social media, compete with the power we gain from opening an envelope and unfolding a piece of paper to reveal a perfectly imperfect voice—words carefully formed by the very pulse of the sender's heartbeat? Letters are artefacts of an embodied mind because the pen is continuously held, the shapes on paper carefully formed, and the reciprocity between thought and action entirely seamless. So, while we can communicate using mechanical and virtual tools, the handwritten letter is most perfect of all.

Lord, turn us towards your grace so that our lives are handwritten letters of love to you.

Amen

LETTERS *for* CHRISTIANS

2
SHOPPING CART

Shopping trips are important for all the different things we need to survive, and at the end of it all there are bags full of our decisions waiting to be checked out. Most of the decisions are automated responses to needs as we've trawled the aisles in boredom. It's an experience similar to a life without CHRIST—full of the same godless behaviour and when it's time for us to check out it's guaranteed to be a truly underwhelming experience. The challenge for Christians is to think of life in terms of what we should be loading into our trolley because what we take from life reflects who we are. We live as servants of GOD and our trolley should be full of HIS decisions.

Lord, help us to shop for the right things in life and give us the wisdom to know what to get and when.

Amen

EVERYDAY LOVE

3
TEACHER

We tend to think the most important teachers are the ones who've had the biggest impact on our lives. Perhaps it's someone who looked after us as a child or at school. Someone who helped our career or saved us from disaster. Watching someone die produces an unforgettable lesson too. In all these moments we were taught valuable lessons and the point about all these teachers is that they existed in that moment of need. In one sense, the biggest lesson is in how fleeting their input has been. They've each also been taught in the same way as we have but we're often unsighted by these networks of meaning. And when these earthly teachers fall silent and their lessons are forgotten in our own haste back into this world there is one teacher who never falls silent. No matter how hard we try our conscience can't hide.

Holy Spirit, don't stop teaching us, we pray, because without you the lessons we've learnt are all meaningless.

Amen

LETTERS *for* CHRISTIANS

4
HEAVENLY

Think
Write
Wait

Think
Read
Wait
Think
Write
Wait

Think

Prayers to our heavenly father are handwritten letters and often short like The Lord's Prayer. There are many of them because it's a conversation. It's not about how many words we can fit in but the thought and care behind them.

Father, we pray for wisdom to think and we pray for courage to write to you— and to wait, thinking about what we've written.

Amen

EVERYDAY LOVE

5
A LURE

Sinful behaviour demands one more thing from us beyond the sin itself: the postponement of thought. That's the trap because if we don't think further than the sin itself, the hold it has over us increases with time. It's a mousetrap or fishing lure. Not fronting up to our sinful nature increases our vulnerability to satanic attack.

Lord, we pray for the ability, every time we sin, to write a letter to ourselves—a sinner's letter—and have it posted without delay to the foot of the cross.

Amen

LETTERS *for* CHRISTIANS

6
WRITERS

We leave behind many forms of letter writing. Shared experiences are unusual 'letters' but so too are things like gravestone inscriptions and epitaphs. They all bear messages. Some messages are felt, others are words but they're all artefacts of communication and can therefore be read just as a handwritten letter can. Especially for those of us left behind, we're able to read them over and over again. Christians should strive to become valuable letter writers because it's a testimony of faith kept, hope endured, and love conveyed.

Lord, help us to be authors of valuable letters, so that the workings of the Holy Spirit in our lives can be passed on with meaning to others.

Amen

EVERYDAY LOVE

7
MOLEHILLS

When relations between people become so bad that the problems created appear to be insurmountable it's often best to give the people involved all the space in the world. 'Moving their minds' adds perspective with the result that problems can become meaningless in the context of the wider world. Christians often feel a need to get involved when that's exactly what our enemy wants. Slow down, breathe, stretch out your arm towards the real problems—and be quiet.

Lord, help us to know when to be quiet.

Amen

LETTERS *for* CHRISTIANS

8
DIRECTNESS

A face so ruddy and wooden that the tobacco pipe was always perfectly camouflaged; only ever revealed by puffs of smoke. His head was more focused than even his eyes, unrelenting in its gaze, as if one's gaze could be completely channelled through the directness and tilt of a head. Who needs eyes when you're as direct as this man was. If OUR LORD had made a most honest man surely this man was evidence of that. And in his hands the folds of sunburnt skin declared that honesty with a booming voice that didn't need a mouth. There are people who are so tough they're gentle. Gentle toughness. There is much joy to be had from our differences that THE LORD must surely delight when HE casts his eye over us all—HIS servants—glorious believers resplendent in our differences and united through HIS grace.

Lord, let us, each as different as we are from one another, seek out your grace.

Amen

EVERYDAY LOVE

9
SECRETS

When we look at art we look for secret messages. It's the special allure of visually investing in objects such as paintings and sculptures. By reading letters just as we do works of art we're rewarded by something that no-one else knows about and our salvation through CHRIST is an experience of a personal relationship that is like no other. Each of us has been rescued differently yet HIS grace is always the same: it's the treasure beyond all treasures.

Lord, help us to hold fast to everything you tell us. Grant us the courage to reveal to all what it is we treasure.

Amen

LETTERS *for* CHRISTIANS

10
HOMEWARD

When we think about planes we often think about them coming in to land. It's that feeling as they slowly descend out from the sky. Taking off—to disappear as they evaporate into the atmosphere—is another way of thinking about planes. Both, of course, are destination bound but if we don't want to vanish like a small dot then the idea of greeting a destination as we come in to land is more appealing for many of us. It's analogous to how our spiritual walk must be: coming in to land.

We are all destination bound. Thank you Lord, for your power and grace as we come in to land.

Amen

EVERYDAY LOVE

11
RECOGNISABLE

Life before the invention of photography and the mirror in the early nineteenth century meant we only had an idea of our image as it was reflected in water, a shiny metal object, or from an artist's impression. The better the artist, the more flattering the representation. Now, thanks to technology, our image is so burnt into our psyche that we're able to see ourselves clearly in mind's eye. But the image that GOD sees is not the image we have of ourselves because without the HOLY SPIRIT we're unrecognisable. You see, we have to be born again for GOD to recognise us and no mirror, reflection, artist, camera, or artificial intelligence is capable of recording that image.

Lord, help us to understand the importance of being born again; it's so that you're able to recognise us.

Amen

LETTERS *for* CHRISTIANS

12
INNOCENCE

Childhood dreams don't stray too far from things like being let loose in a chocolate factory, becoming a world famous sporting hero, or being able to talk to animals. JESUS loved children, partly perhaps because they dream with such ease and innocence. Being born again is an act which returns us to a childlike state, free of pride. We're asked to take those baby steps again as we learn to cope with the world in a different way, one requiring discernment in all matters to do with Christian faith, hope, and love. Accepting that JESUS died for our sins is our testimony of a return to innocence and so we're free to once again dream innocently, even as we mature in faith.

Lord, thank you that we too can call you Father.

Amen

EVERYDAY LOVE

13
CRISIS

The saying that we shouldn't let a crisis go to waste can be interpreted in two ways. A crisis in our lives can be used to wake us up from a situation that may have ended badly if we'd continued our lives in the same way. On the other hand, the manipulation of events as a result of some declared crisis may lead us into a worse situation than before. Our job as Christians is to use a crisis to wake up from whatever slumber we might have been caught up in, or are heading towards.

Lord, help us to see the world for what it is and to never let a crisis go to waste if we're to be useful in your kingdom—for your power and glory, forever and ever.

Amen

LETTERS *for* CHRISTIANS

14
REFLECTION

It's true in a Zen sense of an eagle flying over a lake, that neither the eagle nor the lake intend to influence the other. The eagle doesn't intend to be reflected in the water while the water doesn't intend to reflect the image of the eagle, and yet we're able to enjoy the beauty of these interactions. This world was made for us by our heavenly father so that we may see HIS glorious works and praise HIM for HIS goodness.

Lord may we be forever grateful for how we're able to enjoy what you intended for us.

Amen

EVERYDAY LOVE

15
PICTURES

One birthday card received was a simple hand-drawn picture of the family dog. It's one of the most meaningful letters received and the sender can be seen in all the details, in the lines, shading, and dog's expression. It says *Happy Birthday* more than words can and is a perfect example of why Christians should write more letters; because the more we look at them, the more we think.

Lord, your letter to us is Life
 —and our letter back to you should be: life well lived.

Amen

LETTERS *for* CHRISTIANS

16
PATIENCE

One of the biggest social problems lies in people's judgement of others simply because they don't understand them. It's as if to understand someone else requires supernatural powers, which is really only true if we're talking at the same time. But we do have one superpower: the power of prayer. Prayer is like taking one step back so that we can take two steps forward in our relationships with others.

Lord, we pray the kind of patience which only your Spirit can provide—and then to be patient.

Amen

EVERYDAY LOVE

17
WORRY MERCHANTS

Worry is the world's way of caring. It's a self-fulfilling prophecy because the more we worry the more we feel part of the business of worry. And it's a business with a price tag. The greater the scarcity the more intense the levels of worry and the greater the mark-up, the greater our own perceived value because it reflects our own level of participation. It's a false economy. The more the world tries to sell itself to us the greater the lie because it's not the owner of anything. Nothing we think we buy or invest in, in this world, is ours. This false economy extends into the social world too. It's not only about how we do business but in how we build relationships because people even worry about the levels of worry in other people.

Lord, grant us the peace that only your Spirit can provide so that we don't participate in the false economy of worry.

Amen

LETTERS *for* CHRISTIANS

18
UNSEEN

We should try to remember the people that we don't remember. It's a strange suggestion to make but it should come as no surprise that forgotten people are often the kind of people close to THE LORD'S heart. It may be that we unsee people if we're repulsed by some or other perceived weakness but we also know how, when we're weak, THE LORD is strong. So, the challenge must be to become more aware of the unseen because that's where the power of GOD lies.

Lord, open our eyes to the unseen needs around us.

Amen

EVERYDAY LOVE

19
SPIRITUAL HEALTH

Twice a year we take our car in for a service and our pets get checked out by a vet. Dentist, doctors, psychiatrists, optometrists, audiologists, cancer screening tests, blood tests, you name it, even our smoke alarms are checked every year. When it comes to our faith though we seem to be a little shy. For a start where would we even get faith tested and how would it work? Fortunately for us we needn't worry because THE LORD has got us covered. We'll be tested at exactly the right moment and we just need to tune in for the results.

Lord, you care for sinners like us and know when to test us so that we remain spiritually healthy.

Amen

LETTERS *for* CHRISTIANS

20
FALLEN

We can never tell what a tree really looks like until its leaves have fallen off. What's left is an odd arrangement of trunk and branch bent and twisted by upward travelling nutrients. If a tree's leaves are like fine clothes sparkling in a light breeze for everyone to see then in CHRIST we are glorious trees full of leaves reaching out in all directions; full of HIS grace. It's when we stray that we're revealed in the brokenness and emptiness of this world, like the twisted bark against a cold winter sky.

Lord, may we be like trees full of leaves that sing to your power and majesty.

Amen

EVERYDAY LOVE

21
LOFTY HEIGHTS

Views from a mountain are always inspiring and we often urge ourselves to climb up just to soak in the solitude—watching out over wild air currents, soaring eagles, and rustling vegetation, towards distant scenes. In its exteriority, it's easy to gaze at the landscape with a feeling of power over vast swathes of geometry below but at some point the feeling always turns uneasily inward. A creeping sense of alienation settles over us because we're cut off from people. Our work is meant to be among people—that's where GOD wants us to be. While it's good to climb a mountain every now and again to be refreshed and get some perspective, we don't belong in its silent world. We belong in the tapestry of people woven into the landscape below—because the good news of our salvation must be sewn into place.

Lord, we belong, not to lofty heights divorced from people, but to where your will is to be done—here where your people are being gathered.

Amen

LETTERS *for* CHRISTIANS

22
SPOT IN A LOT

When driving into a huge parking lot, regardless of how many empty spaces there are, we always tend to head to the same spot. It's just one of those things. We feel comfortable in a certain zone parked in a certain space. You could say it's because we're closer to a certain shop or doorway but there's a sense of familiarity at play here. We like to stick to doing things we've done before. There's a danger in that approach sometimes if we depend on the familiar for our reality or world view. Often Christians are asked to embrace the unfamiliar, the uncomfortable, or the unwanted. So, every now and then let's park in a different spot.

Guide us Lord to what you want us to see and show us what you need us to do, we pray with thanksgiving.

Amen

EVERYDAY LOVE

23
MISMATCH

How we clothe ourselves says a lot about us. It's not a sin to wear clothing that reflects who we are but it is if we depend on that image for validation from people around us. That's the trap which produces an identity crisis in us—the mismatch between who we are and what we're projecting. Our job isn't to impress man, it's to write those *letters* announcing forgiveness of sins, not through our own efforts or image making, but through HIS grace. So, let's simply be recognisable for what GOD has done for us through OUR LORD JESUS CHRIST.

Lord, we're reminded again of who we are and in whose image we're made. Help us to be your living servant and not a slave to this world.

Amen

LETTERS *for* CHRISTIANS

24
PROGRESSION

There are channels on YouTube that celebrate past events, where people participate in interviews as they recount events from their unique perspective. The results either converge or diverge from recorded history and we're sometimes left wondering whether looking back does us any good. The past appears to be helpful if it has a positive impact on the way we approach the future because we should learn not only from our mistakes but also from what we did right. The story of JESUS is a case in point because we grow in faith by revisiting HIS story and finding common threads between the Old and New Testament. The interviews we enjoy are with THE HOLY SPIRIT who provides all the wisdom we need to understand the past and our role in the future.

Lord, may your past give life to us all, through the power of your Holy Spirit.

Amen

EVERYDAY LOVE

25
OUR SHADOW

Some things follow us around everywhere. Our reputation, our unacknowledged sins, and even in moonlight we have a presence beyond our bodies. It's our shadow. Our reputation follows us like a shadow, so too sin that remains undealt with. A shadow leaves everything it touches intact and yet leaves nothing unchanged. Standing in someone's way blocks their sun or darkens their view; which is why we should always be aware of any shadow we're casting. There are people in our lives who we may have affected negatively because we haven't been aware of our indirect effect on them, for example, when we've been in the limelight, talked over them, misrepresented them, or ignored them.

Lord, make us aware of people around us and help us to give them a voice when they most need it.

Amen

LETTERS *for* CHRISTIANS

26
ALARM BELLS

Every day has something to teach us. Huddled in a corner of the lobby in the early hours one winter's morning was a person who appeared to be in distress. But it wasn't as bad as it looked. They'd locked themselves out and were waiting for a locksmith. The lesson for those of us who walk past, is that often *we're* the emergency because we don't notice or care enough to find out how serious a situation might be. We often misread an emergency because we assume it's someone else who needs help when in fact the alarm bells are ringing for us: for being dismissive, cold, or disassociated from a scene unfolding right in front of our eyes.

Father, we pray for eyes that see and ears that hear, for wisdom to understand and compassion to help in whatever way possible.

Amen

EVERYDAY LOVE

27
BETRAYAL

Have we ever thought about something we've done and wondered whether it was worth it? Spare a thought for the utter desolation in the mind of Judas when he looked at those coins and it all started to sink in. Did he try to conjure up some warmth from the inert image in front of him? Was there any warmth in the room when he was handed his reward? Some 2,000 years later can we be found guilty of handing JESUS over? Have we, when pushed, denied knowing JESUS? These are not easy thoughts to have but we should be mindful at all times what our thoughts and actions in the company of men actually mean.

Lord, we're wretched without you. Let us stand firm in your grace when approached by people seeking praise and respect when there is none to give.

Amen

LETTERS *for* CHRISTIANS

28
IDOLS IN US

We're all now used to seeing faces buried in mobile phones. It's a good tactic when on a narrow pathway, to pretend we're absorbed by something important on the phone as we barrel our way through the crowd. The threat isn't so much that we're now expected to answer a call or message within milliseconds but in what it's doing to our spiritual well-being. Technology has introduced a false god: us. We've begun worshipping ourselves. This fascination with our own image has reached such intolerable levels of deception in society that we can expect GOD to turn away in disgust.

Lord, pull us away from the trap laid.

Amen

EVERYDAY LOVE

29
THE TUBE

The London Underground or 'Tube' is a fascinating network connecting people with places overhead. If we had X-ray vision we'd be able to watch from the sky as it snakes its way around the city. The overwhelming sensation we have while hurtling along its noisy track is one of resignation. We're resigned to the direction of travel and there's no let up until the next stop, nothing to be done but wait. It's the same in a plane except underground feels creepier as people are jammed in, lights flicker and sparks fly. If there's one curious thing about the Tube it's how people avoid making eye contact. So, what we experience are dystopian bursts of anti-social disorientation going one way—but some people love it.

Help us Lord to love people in all sorts of situations, whether we're on a plane or in the Tube, it matters not for we're there with you.

Amen

LETTERS *for* CHRISTIANS

30
USE OF US

It's difficult to imagine a park bench in any other setting where the affordance it offers is not to be sat on. Other objects have scores of uses. Books have uses which are limited only by the mind, through the stories contained within them. They can even be stacked to support a shelf or used as a doorstop. But we humans are the most useful of all things which is probably why we're targeted in some way or other. In a political and socio-economic sense we're valuable for countless reasons: military, marketing, to experiment on, in health matters, religion, the economy, indoctrination, education, social structures, and psychological manipulation. But for GOD we have only one use which is to glorify HIM—having been made in HIS image, and saved through HIS grace.

We don't wish to be useful in any other way Lord, than to glorify your name.

Amen

EVERYDAY LOVE

31
FRIENDS

There are friends and there are *friends*. We can strike up a conversation with some friends after years of being apart; as if we'd seen them yesterday. Others are people we might hardly ever have spoken to but are friends because both families shared a deep and enduring history together. Then there are those friends who've passed away and yet every time we think about them they seem to be on their way over to visit or having just said goodbye. There are also friends we've never met. Often called pen pals these are the type of friends who we know through letter writing or things like online listservs and forums that bring people with similar interests together. As Christians we see CHRIST as a friend, even though we've never met or spoken to HIM in the traditional sense of the word—and yet we have met HIM and spoken to HIM. Our meeting was when we were born again and we speak through our prayers.

Our Saviour is most special of all, for He knew us before we were even born.

Amen

LETTERS *for* CHRISTIANS

32
CHOICE

For some people who've stayed in one place all their lives there's a spirit of restlessness, of wishing they'd travelled more. Then there are people who have travelled the globe who sometimes wished they'd stayed in one place. There are advantages to both lifestyles and the decision is ours: to travel and explore or to consolidate and build. For both scenarios the only requirement of us is that we build towards THE KINGDOM OF GOD. Staying in one place produces a certain type of Christian while another type of Christian is formed from exploration but both pathways lead to the same destination: where we're born again.

Lord, however we've journeyed through this life it's always been the destination that was important: You.

Amen

EVERYDAY LOVE

33
GOOGLY

Christians need to be savvy to the cult of enforcement that has taken hold in many of our churches. The cult demands certain rights transcend others which is impossible because behaviour is not a performance which can be privileged. Denominations have evolved in Christianity because we're all *different*, not all *right*. If we don't agree with someone, we move along or we allow them to move on. A person who wants to subjugate others to their world view isn't a Christian. The Jews themselves were free to choose a human king against GOD'S warnings. Yet, despite the mercy of GOD, the church in recent times has seen fit to privilege behaviour which contradicts THE BIBLE. In a cricket match with the church batting the commentary would be—OUT! Bowled by a googly! We can only hope for a better 2nd innings from these churches.

Lord, inspire our church leaders and give them courage to follow your truth.

Amen

LETTERS *for* CHRISTIANS

34
TWO SEE

A car's headlights are used by the driver to see in poor conditions but they're also there to be seen. Some of us are preoccupied with using GOD's word to see out into the darkness during times of trial as difficulties descend on our lives. Others are focused on being that lamp on a stand for all to see. In deteriorating conditions both groups are important but we're especially useful when we act together.

Lord, help us to seek you out with the light of your word as well as to be a light for those seeking you.

Amen

EVERYDAY LOVE

35
TWO NEEDS

Everyone has at some point engaged in the hypothetical about which of their moving parts they would sacrifice if they were forced to. Many of us feel we'd be able to cope without our hearing, some prefer to be without sight, or taste, or perhaps we'd be prepared to loose one of our limbs if it meant everything else remained in good working order. The family of CHRIST, GOD'S church, must also sometimes decide on how best to cope with leadership issues or where spiritual gifts are absent from the congregation. Even in Christian homes we struggle against each other as we try to establish whose needs are more pressing. An elderly widow's needs are always more important especially when it comes to physical and spiritual care.

Lord, may we always choose wisely and act lovingly as members of the family of Christ.

Amen

LETTERS *for* CHRISTIANS

36
MISFITS

Buying clothes is one of those things we either love or hate. There's nothing quite like standing in a fitting room with hangers bashing around as one item of clothing after another goes flying. Crouch, bend, step back, sideways, bang our head, jump up and down, squint, squat, tie, untie, bang an elbow, organise the piles into keep and return, confuse the piles, look for another size, another colour, return to the fitting room, and repeat. The problem for many of us is that we can't relate to a lot of the clothing in the first place so the search between stores is even more mentally taxing. Once we were misfits in this world but it's no longer a problem when we're born again because there's no need to ever go back into that fitting room.

Lord, we may be misfits here in this world but not in your kingdom.

Amen

EVERYDAY LOVE

37
SOUP

Soup kitchens are often synonymous with virtue signalling but despite this negative connotation, are hard to argue against. Feeding the poor and destitute is an act of compassion and will always be noticed by the LORD wherever it occurs. Sometimes, however, we forget about those spiritual soup kitchens which are not so obvious and which are not easily hijacked by attention seekers such as politicians. GOD'S church is one of the more obvious spiritual soup kitchens. Its primary role is to gather and minister to all in search of THE LORD. Bible study groups are another. The most important soup kitchen may even be in our next door neighbour's house or, if we look hard enough, at a train station or bus stop on our way to work.

Lord, may there be a spiritual soup kitchen wherever the downtrodden and poor in spirit are.

Amen

LETTERS *for* CHRISTIANS

38
PAGE TURNERS

The keyboard of a computer is an interesting device. If we want the word 'love' we have to summon it by pressing four buttons. It's always the same buttons and then nothing happens except for a word which appears on our screen. This world demands we be button pushers. That's the way it loves us. A button is pushed when we're born, we press a button to get a school report, then an offer of employment, a marriage certificate, a will, doctor's reports—and then all of a sudden we stop pressing buttons. When we open our Bible and want the word 'love' there are only pages to turn. When we turn those pages a word appears in our hearts: JESUS. What we need to do is to stop pressing buttons and start turning pages.

Lord, help us to be better page turners so that when our race is run we're just turning the page.

Amen

EVERYDAY LOVE

39
HAMBURGER

"Hamburger!" most of us have shouted at least once in our lives as levels of anticipation have gone through the roof. It's a thing we've worshipped but what's the message and why are we so smitten by this food? The reason must be the same as it is for everything in the world: a false promise. "See how this world satisfies you, it's yours, you can have it forever if you submit to me" we're told. JESUS experienced the same temptation from the devil who didn't even make what he was offering, just spoilt it. It's perhaps the biggest threat to modern-day Christianity, along with the promise of convenience. "Eat this, it's available within seconds" we're told. And it's not a far cry from that infamous incident with an 'apple.' It's as fleeting too. Within ten minutes we're hungry again.

Lord, keep us from straying beyond the only true promise made, that if we repent and are born again we will know your love.

Amen

LETTERS *for* CHRISTIANS

40
ALWAYS ON

A light switch. Now there's something that's taken for granted. We switch it on to see and switch it off when light is no longer needed. Sometimes we forget to switch it off but we never forget to switch it on. We are like that sometimes (forgetting that it's on) but when we're having a crisis, and it's off, we reach for that switch very quickly. When we're at war the churches are full, people start singing, the mood is reflective and sincere. Even soldiers how soldiers become believers when the bullets start flying. There's nothing wrong with this behaviour as we seek relief from what's befallen us but let's try to remember that the light is always on, unless we've turned it off on purpose.

Lord, may your light be our guide.

Amen

EVERYDAY LOVE

41
BE DRESSED

Having to wear glasses is always a bit of a pain but we've got no choice if we want to be able to see properly. There are some Christians who need to see properly but who refuse to. They see what they saw fifty years ago and for them that's good enough. But what's in front of them now isn't how it was fifty years ago and it's important for every Christian to be able to recognise the enemy today. So, they should have their eyes tested, order a sturdier frame and get dressed in GOD'S armour if they wish to understand the world today because we're to be properly dressed when HE returns.

Lord, help us to see the enemy properly.

Amen

LETTERS *for* CHRISTIANS

42
FARMING

There's a saying that we don't grow grapes, we provide the conditions for grapes to grow. For Christians, the right conditions mean we work on relationships, we work on our prayers, and we try to set a good example because we know people watch us to know more about GOD. But creating the right conditions is like farming. It takes time, effort and patience.

Lord, help us to become part of the right conditions to grow your kingdom.

Amen

EVERYDAY LOVE

43
LAYERS

The main purpose of any building is for shelter and protection and there's a point reached during construction when a building meets these needs. Then comes the layering. We paint the walls, doors, and ceilings or stick laminate down on the floors. We tile surfaces and decorate entrances. We don't need this layering for shelter or protection but, because we want to say something more about ourselves, we do it anyway. Sometimes we go a little too far and what we say and do isn't really who we are. It's a trap which is easy to fall into and is worth pointing out if we come across a brother or sister with a layering problem.

Keep us humble Lord, and correct us when trying to be someone we're not.

Amen

LETTERS *for* CHRISTIANS

44
LIFE GOES ON

The calm of a beautiful peaceful crisp morning filled with birdsong was suddenly shattered by automatic gunfire. The firing continued for a couple of minutes and then stopped just as suddenly. A soldier recounts how the strangest thing about the whole ordeal was that the birds kept on singing. Sometimes we wonder at the lack of warmth around us, at how cold and disassociated the world can be in times of distress, as life just seems to go on paying no mind. It's a lesson for some that nature isn't love. Nor are buildings, mobile phones or anything else we often covet. Only GOD is.

Only you, Lord, can teach us what love is. Everything else follows a pathway towards alienation and indifference.

Amen

EVERYDAY LOVE

45
SMALL GARDEN

Some people have a pot plant for their garden. Others have a balcony or tiny backyard. Then there are those bigger gardens that are the envy of many. The one thing about a small garden is that we tend to notice everything. We see the same returning visitors such as a bee or finch. We also know when a plant needs water or has too much. It's the same for congregations. Often the best congregations are small. We don't need stadiums for churches, we just need groups of articulate, thoughtful, caring people to spread the good news of salvation—who know how much prayer is needed for each of us to grow. Lots of small gardens make for lots of happy people.

Plant us in a small garden Lord, so that we may grow to our full potential.

Amen

LETTERS *for* CHRISTIANS

46
NEXT TO US

When we look at something, what we see is *our view* of it. We can't see what's behind it or what it looks like from another angle so we need to move to get more information. If it's a distant object then we have to make do with the picture that we see. Our lives are like that. We have to keep moving to understand the context we're in and sometimes we're quite a distance away from understanding an important event or experience. If we look out into the night sky to appreciate how small we are it's easy to forget that GOD is right next to us, not millions of miles away.

Right next to you Lord, is where we want to be.

Amen

EVERYDAY LOVE

47
YOU ARE HERE

It's useful to know where we are when looking at a map. Then again, in another sense, we are here in this book, about halfway through. Some people would love to know where they are in their lives except it would mean they'll know the day of their passing. The Bible too doesn't let us know where we are in a temporal sense but we have an idea from prophecies that are left to be fulfilled. Still, that gives us no indication about the length of time left before the LORD's return described in Revelation. *You are here* is really all we need to know because, yes, we are here, at this point in time—and with good reason. But each one of us is here for only a very short time so let's focus on being here—now—and let GOD take care of everything else.

Lord, thank you that we're here now. Grant us the wisdom to know why it's we who are now here.

Amen

LETTERS *for* CHRISTIANS

48
A TORCH

For some, this world is a pail of water. They put their hand in hoping that when they take it out again it will have made a difference. Too late they realise they've made no difference at all—the water appears as glassy and unperturbed as ever. GOD'S true church on the other hand is not a pail of water. It's a shining light which gets brighter with every believer's torch.

Thank you Lord that our torches, however weak, are able to make a difference in your kingdom.

Amen

EVERYDAY LOVE

49
RISEN SON

Not a single person would disagree that there's a huge difference between a sunrise and a sunset—even though one's just a reversal of the other. But it's not the sun that's different; it's *we* who are the difference because we're not the same people at the beginning and end of a day. Our minds are pointed outwards in the morning—goal oriented—while in the evening they're inward looking, reflective as we get ready to draw the curtains. It's just that we see the atmosphere in a different light. Believers also experience this change in spiritual mindset where, when guided by THE HOLY SPIRIT, we perform our worship through outward acts of faith and, at other times, inwardly through prayer.

For us, Christ has risen all of our days.

Amen

LETTERS *for* CHRISTIANS

50
WHEN WE GET IT

There can't be anyone who, having received a bicycle for Christmas, has looked for the operator's manual. We all just jumped straight on and started pedalling. After crashing numerous times we finally get it and there's no stopping us. It's the same with being born again. There are also plenty of crashes and lots of tears but one day we just get it—and the rest is history.

When we get it, we really get it! Thank you Lord, for helping us to see.

Amen

EVERYDAY LOVE

51
OBSTACLE RACE

The earth is so full of obstacles compared to the sky that obstacles must be good for us because they teach us to go around, over, under, or through them. But even if we're in an environment with no obstacles we'd still have a problem—because most of the time *we're* the obstacle. We're our own greatest enemy, so full of sin that we can't escape. We're mentally trapped. The only way out is to be born again.

Open our eyes Lord, that we may be free of our greatest obstacle: ourselves.

Amen

LETTERS *for* CHRISTIANS

52
IMAGE MAKERS

Product brands are everywhere. They're markers of ownership and exclusivity. But these elite clubs, which we're invited to join, come at a price. Some brands have become so powerful that ownership no longer lies in the product but in us. We are owned, firstly by way of a benign electronic registration—a marking of territory if you will. Then we become part of an image but the trouble with becoming an image is that we're no longer real. In the grand scheme of things we're just another product: expendable.

Lord, may we resist the temptation to become a product of this world.

Amen

EVERYDAY LOVE

53
IMAGE TAKERS

A potter doesn't look right in a chef's hat. A car mechanic won't impress dressed as a nun. There's an expectation that needs to be matched in the image we have of things. We also don't expect to see a church minister dressed up in a Halloween costume. Whenever we see Christian faith dressed inappropriately we should take note because it's a sign that the representation is done on purpose, intended to disrupt GOD's laws. It's a sign of the devil doing what the devil enjoys doing.

We pray for wisdom Lord, because what the way we dress says about us, it really means to say about you.

Amen

LETTERS *for* CHRISTIANS

54
AMID THE NOISE

Many a dog has been sent into a state of sheer terror at the sound of a dragster testing their engine out on a quiet suburban street. Then there are fireworks which have exactly the same effect. At the opposite end of the spectrum, soft noises are sometimes just as scary as loud bangs. The great thing about being a Christian is that GOD doesn't need to attract our attention in this way. What we need to do to be saved, is most plainly stated, exquisitely clear, and eye watering in its directness.

Lord, we don't fear men because we fear you more.

Amen

EVERYDAY LOVE

55
LIVING WATER

Water, water everywhere ... (in bottles, that is). Some of us are old enough to remember life when tap water from a reservoir or stream was all we needed. It was drinkable and free. It's now a commercial enterprise and expensive. Water is symbolically important and metaphorically relevant. We're baptised in water to signify the freedom we gain. It's the life giving force which the HOLY SPIRIT makes known to us. The ransom has been paid. Hallelujah!

Thank you Lord for giving us the water of life.

Amen

LETTERS *for* CHRISTIANS

56
TRAFFIC LIGHTS

Traffic lights are useful if you like following rules. They are great for people who like taking orders without thinking. Cities install them to create order and yet many other cities rely on people's common sense by using a broad framework of social cues. One of the biggest issues JESUS had was how the religious elite used a system of traffic lights—or rules—to suppress and exclude HIS people from growing spiritually. What we all need to decide on for ourselves is what kind of believer we'd like to be, one that loves to obey rules such as the laws of the Old Testament, or one who loves the freedom of the New Testament and understands what being born again really means. Going forward, this decision alone will help separate the wheat from the chaff.

Lord, you came to break the chains that enslave us. We are now new creatures in your sight.

Amen

EVERYDAY LOVE

57
LIFE

GOD'S creation is amazing. No two faces are identical, no tree or leaf is the same, blade of grass, animal, bird, fish, insect, grain of sand, hairs on our head: not one is identical to the other. By comparison, man can make stuff which is identical especially in components that go into making things like toys, furniture, cars, or aircraft. They have to be precise copies to fit properly. But the more important difference is that GOD'S creation has life while man's has none.

Lord, may you forgive our arrogance and pride. Fill us with humility because you Lord are the creator of heaven and earth and all that is in it.

Amen

LETTERS *for* CHRISTIANS

58
DEPTH OF TIME

Flights are interesting experiences because of what our mind doesn't do. While we're being physically catapulted across the globe our mind stays in one place. It's not moving at all. Our bodies know they're moving fast but our mind belongs in another dimension. We can speculate about what the difference is between mind and body as we experience how space might be different to time. If we say that space is depth of time then things start to make more sense. Our body is moving fast through the air, i.e. space. But the mind is not space but time, so the mind is a constant that remains in one place. GOD's bride, the church is scattered over the earth but our minds are all in one place: GOD's hands. That's the difference—and one day time will give way to another dimension: eternity.

Lord, wherever we physically are, our minds are always grounded in one place: your love. It never changes just as you never change.

Amen

EVERYDAY LOVE

59
SIDEWALK

A pavement or sidewalk is the same as a street or road in many ways. We try not to bump into each other and we keep to the space provided. The difference is in the type of movement we're engaged in. Streets are full of fast moving 'capsules' containing people who are completely cut off and disengaged from life around them. Pavements, on the other hand, are full of life. There might be chairs and tables, dogs on leads, and people of all ages and nationalities. It's the kind of space that the LORD loves because HE can make a difference if people slow down enough. A sidewalk slows us all down and forces us to be closer together.

Lord, help us to slow down on life's sidewalks because they're full of people with different needs. May we not ignore them by living our lives in the fast lane.

Amen

LETTERS *for* CHRISTIANS

60
DISTORTION

How many of us can say when we take a photograph that the final image was exactly what we had in mind? Most of the time we see new opportunities in an image that we'd not originally seen when standing there at the scene, camera in hand. How others interpret the image also means it's a different image from the original. It therefore makes sense to be cautious in the way we handle information so that we know the difference between the original scene and how it's later framed. It's even more important as Christians that we resist the temptation to distort the word of GOD.

Lord, may we forever know your truth and resist the temptation to reinterpret your message to us simply because it looks 'nicer' or 'fits in' with our earthly goals or desires.

Amen

EVERYDAY LOVE

61
SOCIAL RULES

Teatime is a special occasion for many and usually takes place around mid-morning or mid-afternoon. These kind of social rules are not imposed on us but grow on us to the point that they can become quite inflexible. There are many other examples of how we structure society using 'rules' that don't really have a logic to them. It's through CHRIST THAT we no longer have to be concerned with man-made rules. So, next time a brother or sister wants to impose a set of rules it's easy to see through what it is they're actually trying to do. GOD doesn't want people to worship HIM because there's a rule that says so. Instead HE delights in being worshipped because *we really want to worship* our SAVIOUR and KING.

Lord, thank you for lifting the burden from us at the cross.

Amen

LETTERS *for* CHRISTIANS

62
A LID

Modern-day life has a lid for everything which disgusts us. General rubbish falls into this category including laundry baskets, kitchen bins, refuse bins, and wastewater. In biblical times salt was used as 'a lid' to cover over offensive material. When we're asked to 'put a lid on it' we know exactly what's meant. Lids are there to hide things but they can also be opened. What CHRIST did was to reveal what man didn't want GOD to see. Trying to hide from GOD is a futile exercise. CHRIST came to unhide offensive, hypocritical behaviour so that all men may see—and be saved.

Lord, open our eyes to the hypocrites, liars, and thieves so that we may see them for who they really are.

Amen

EVERYDAY LOVE

63
SOLID GROUND

Roots hold a tree up and foundations hold a house up. Both are hidden. What holds us up as people are our forefathers and how we've been taught by them directly or indirectly. They too are now hidden in time. Some cultures stand on solid ground while others fall. Those that remain standing are like trees and buildings on solid ground. It's the one thing we have in common that makes a difference: solid ground.

We're on solid ground if we've accepted Jesus as Lord and Saviour.

Amen

LETTERS *for* CHRISTIANS

64
REST

Any demanding undertaking such as building a house or writing a book is followed by a period of rest. But what exactly does rest mean? Sleep? Yes, sometimes, but it also means that we disengage for a while. It may be just sitting back and looking at the book lying on the bookshelf or unwinding in the garden of a new house. We should follow GOD'S example when HE rested as HE watched over HIS marvellous creation. Such is the importance of rest.

Lord, if it be your will, may we be well rested so that we're well grounded in your word.

Amen

EVERYDAY LOVE

65
WORDS

Words matter. The meaning of those words matter more. What matters most however is what your heart, not your mouth, is saying. We're all guilty of rushed prayers because we're 'busy' or in a 'bad mood.' Maybe we're feeling sick or late for a meeting. There are a million reasons to be in a hurry when it's time talk to GOD but it's better to say a few words with our whole heart than to rattle off a meaningless rushed prayer.

Lord, may our prayers be less hasteful and more meaningful.

Amen

LETTERS *for* CHRISTIANS

66
LOOKING GOOD

Things like brushing our teeth, washing our hair, using deodorant, putting on clean clothes and generally being presentable, are important to most of us. It doesn't need to get done but the social consequences are pretty severe if we don't do it. Does it make a difference to GOD? Not in the least, because GOD weighs our heart, not what we present as our image.

Lord, remind us that we're washed in your mercy, not in the things that make us look good.

Amen

EVERYDAY LOVE

67
TRUE LOVE

For most of us the biggest fear is to be without love—that we're either not loved or we don't love. There can't be a situation more heartbreaking than to be without love and yet it's the easiest thing in the world to fix.

We who seek love must find God through Christ—for there is no greater love than the precious love of Christ.

Amen

LETTERS *for* CHRISTIANS

68
PUBS AND POLICE

There's a pub around the corner claiming to date back to the 1400s. Now that's a fine bit of history to lay claim to. Many British pubs are full of the most interesting, intelligent people which is especially true if we're in one, because don't we become more interesting too? The secret of course is moderation and this is evidenced in many traditional pubs. Pubs are so well integrated into the social fabric that they have interesting stories to tell. One pub has been known to double up as a courthouse during the day so you've not far to go if you misbehave. But this particular pub's neighbour is a local Christian minister, so you've not far to go if you would like to be saved either. The point about 'pubs' wherever they may be is that it would be wrong to judge everyone in them by painting with the same brush.

Lord, let us not judge lest we be judged.

Amen

EVERYDAY LOVE

69
WE WHO WERE

It's not hard to fall into the trap of thinking that we're part of a superior culture. If anyone's traced their family history back to as far as records allow they may at some point have muttered under their breath about certain events or failings. We might even be tempted to think that people weren't as bright as we are today. That way of thinking is a huge mistake. We've not changed one bit. We're the people JESUS dealt with in HIS day: the same behaviour repeated again today.

Lord may we humble ourselves before you as we realise that we're no better than anyone else before us. You remain our only hope—as you were theirs.

Amen

LETTERS *for* CHRISTIANS

70
FIND LOVE

Robins are one of the cutest birds of all but let's not fool ourselves that because we love them they love us back. Polar bears look cute too but try hugging one. Nor are penguins, squirrels, otters, or anything else that we find endearing in some way or other. The same goes for the images we make such as Disney characters or brands like McDonald's which is essentially just a cheap bun that's not really very good for us. The point here is that no matter how much we want these types of things to be part of our lives, to love us, they don't. Not really. Love is very special and it's not found on television screens, mobile phones, The BBC, cooking shows, or Instagram. It definitely won't be found in artificial intelligence either. If we want to discover what love is we should talk to GOD and the only way to do that is through JESUS. It's only then that we'll understand.

Thank you Lord that we're able to understand love through the sacrifice you made for us on the cross.

Amen

EVERYDAY LOVE

71
EYES ON

Out on a hike, to head for something we can't see we normally find something distinctive to use as a marker. But unless we're very focused it can be easy to lose our bearings. The landscape changes very quickly as we move through it. What we thought was close by ends up being miles in front or behind. What used to be a sharp pointy feature can't be distinguished from the surroundings anymore. A distinctive patch of colour has suddenly become an endless mass of vegetation and we're completely lost. Our walk in faith is not much different. We need to keep our eye on THE CROSS because, as the landscape changes, its easy to lose our way.

Lord, give us wisdom, resolve, and strength of character to run the race and finish at the right destination.

Amen

LETTERS *for* CHRISTIANS

72
TROLLEY TROUBLE

How can we resist thinking about the effect on us of supermarkets and airports. You could land a Boeing in some supermarkets and airports are really just giant supermarkets. And aside from being containers on a grand scale there's one tiny little component in both that test our will to live sometimes: the trolley. Steering those trolleys full of stuff around is probably the worst experience you could have when either jet–lagged or all shopped out. Try steering left, it goes right; try going faster, it catches a wobble; try going quietly, it starts an irritating squeak. Insult it and one wheel stops working. Whatever we try to do with a trolley it does the opposite and we're left feeling deflated. That's the way THE LORD must feel about us sometimes.

Lord, we're far more valuable than a trolley to you so forgive us when we're obstinate in our ways, we pray.

Amen

EVERYDAY LOVE

73
LIFE'S RHYTHM

The rhythm of life can be found everywhere in nature. For us, one person becomes two. Two becomes three, four, and more. We make space for a pet. A room is added, the front lawn extended, a vegetable garden, pool, new car, another new car, more pets, more rooms. Soon we're holding our breath and looking at each other in amazement. How did it come to this we think incredulously. Then, as we slowly let the air out, the youngest finishes school, one car has seized. We trim back the garden and let the 'difficult' spaces become overgrown. The extra rooms are suddenly uncomfortably empty, the last Labrador is wheezing and, as dusk approaches, we exhale softly. *It all goes so fast* we hear ourselves agree. Curtains are drawn. There's a tinkle of two glasses, then one. Our lives are done and what's left is a faint pulse. Almost gone. But memories and joy are passed on—by GOD's grace.

Praise God, for life's rhythm.

Amen

LETTERS *for* CHRISTIANS

74
LITTLE CHILDREN

The rooms of a childhood house are often sacred spaces in our minds. Haven't our eyes traced every square inch, finding a story wherever we looked? Through our windows, in the shadows against the walls, cracks in the plaster, picture frames and peeling paint. If our lives are like rooms then GOD's house is full of them—perfect rooms with wide windows—waiting for HIS children to return. Then each room will be as one—singing with such joy that the angels will applaud GOD's love, wisdom, and mercy.

Lord, we are but children. But we are your children—even if the logic of your ways elude us.

Amen

EVERYDAY LOVE

75
LEAVING

Luggage has no other possible meaning for us than some form of relocation. We look at the buckles, they say *get ready*. The tags mean *look for your keys*. The zip asks *have you got everything?* The flaps want to know, *can you fit anything else in?* It's when the luggage is all neatly stacked (or unceremoniously piled up) that we get that feeling in the pit of our stomach: *the journey is about to begin*. The journey that we most fear is the one we know nothing about: getting ready to leave this world. It's perfectly natural to feel that way because this life is all we've known. The biggest challenge we're asked to confront as Christians is fear—or rather to not fear. We all have to leave sometime but fortunately we get to choose what to pack.

Lord, your mercy and grace are all we need to pack for our journey home.

Amen

LETTERS *for* CHRISTIANS

76
IN TOUCH

Some people used smoke signals, others drums, then came stone tablets, letters, and songs. The way we stay in touch has now moved on as we all become part of a particular throng: The Cloud. Not the clouds we look at to see if it'll rain but the type that clouds the mind because we're now singing a different song. It seems like the more we stay in touch with each other these days the more we feel out of touch. Is it because we've too much to say, when before, staying in touch was a luxury, privilege, and an honour?

Lord, may the words we write and the things we say be enough—not too much.

Amen

EVERYDAY LOVE

77
INVISIBLE

Some of the most important things we interact with are invisible. The wind is, but we can feel it. Noise is, but we can hear it. All we see is the effect of these things on people. They're also completely normal to us and yet some of us have difficulty in understanding that one invisible mighty counsellor: THE HOLY SPIRIT.

Lord, thank you for your Holy Spirit, without which we would be lost forever.

Amen

LETTERS *for* CHRISTIANS

78
SCALE

The things that protrude vertically from the earth all have a scale to them which affects the levels of comfort we experience when we're around them. But there's a point at which the scale of things forces us into a less comfortable relationship with our surroundings. Take trees, for example, which are all comfortably high. Churches with their steeples have historically also been comfortably high. When we get to things like high-rise buildings they appear to be failing us because we're unable to reconcile how high they are with their shape. They may be impressive structures and we may be impressed but that's about it. To be dwarfed by man– made things is unnatural because we've been created by GOD with scale in mind—HIS scale.

Keep us humble Lord we pray, true to scale, because arrogance and pride leads to death.

Amen

EVERYDAY LOVE

79
DIS·[H]·MAY

Satellite dishes are all over the place, pointed up in every direction at satellites everywhere in space pointing down. It's technology that does what it says on the tin, which is for communication and surveillance. But if we don't know what we don't know then how useful is the technology apart from telling us what we already know or doing what we expect it to do. It's technology that would dismay GOD because HE knows what it is we don't know.

Lord, forgive our ignorance because we don't know what we don't know and, more importantly, we don't know what You know.

Amen

LETTERS *for* CHRISTIANS

80
SYNERGY

As a plane flies directly over where we sit on a bench with views over the city, we may think it strange that 1,500 feet or 500 meters directly above is a person sitting in *their* seat thinking about GOD. It would be stranger still if we're both also thinking about GOD at the same time. And in our gaze across the city towards a tower block the same distance away, there might be another person on the 50th floor thinking about GOD. Wouldn't that be wonderfully strange and an inspiration to all three of us if we were all aware in that moment of our thoughts together. How wonderful it will be then when we're all finally reconciled through JESUS and can share in HIS glory together, as one.

Let's take heart in the levels of faith around us because God is full of warmth and compassion.

Amen

EVERYDAY LOVE

81
EVERYWHERE

On buses, vans, trains and buildings—on just about anything that gets in our way—someone's trying to sell us something and it's always urgent. Imagine if instead, every message was replaced by a message from GOD. Perhaps they all are if we care to look. What we sometimes forget is that there are just as many messages from GOD around us—every day—but we just don't see them because of the visual pollution. Many are warnings, but most of them are messages of HIS power and glory because GOD's letters are everywhere for HIS children to see. We should take time to marvel at HIS works.

Thank you Lord, that even as this world deteriorates we see the majesty and splendour of your creation everywhere and every day.

Amen

LETTERS *for* CHRISTIANS

82
TRUST

With the growing number of social problems caused by the unrelenting assault on people's inalienable rights, their dignity, and their faith, the question of the role we're to play becomes critical. There can be no doubt that the best approach to take is the approach that JESUS took when HE was confronted with these social issues. The one thing THE LORD didn't do was to follow orders which went against GOD and nor should we. We have THE HOLY SPIRIT to guide us in the decisions we make about whether what we're being asked (or told) to do, goes against GOD. If it goes against GOD we're not to comply because we're to fear GOD, not man. It really is that simple. We must have courage and trust in GOD no matter what.

Lord, give us courage and strengthen our resolve in days of adversity and trial.

Amen

EVERYDAY LOVE

83
FREEDOM

This is a story about two dogs that are often seen at various times of the day in one of the local parks. The fact that they're dogs and not any other creature is not important to the message being shared here. The first dog is always on a lead and follows orders perfectly but it's not a happy creature and has a nasty streak, getting into fights with little warning. The second dog is almost always off the leash. It's a confident, happy dog that is comfortable around people. It's allowed to bark and its favourite thing is to chase squirrels. Who would we rather have as our master—forced to follow rules or allowed to decide which rules to follow? Which master would we prefer and which owner is happier? JESUS came to save us from the tyranny of man's rules and is happiest when HE sees us happy—GOD-FEARING but happy.

Lord, thank you for your sacrifice which flung open the doors allowing us the freedom to be better servants.

Amen

LETTERS *for* CHRISTIANS

84
LOST

Birds in a flock are a sight to be enjoyed, each one adjusting in milliseconds to its neighbour, continuously connected by the smallest gap of air as the group floats and dives, twists and turns—all at breakneck speed. Hundreds of individuals acting as one. Starlings, especially, form swarms the size of large storm clouds. GOD's real church also acts in this way but at a different scale and intensity. We're more like a flock of sheep, gentle and meek but with the same connection between each other guiding us along. Sheep know their shepherd and a lost sheep is a sight that needs no words. We all get lost in our lives but if we keep calling our shepherd will hear us.

Lord, we're lost until we're born again and from that moment on we know your voice if we ever feel lost again.

Amen

EVERYDAY LOVE

85
& FOUND

Hide and seek is a game every child knows how to play. Watching it played reminds us of how we behave as adults sometimes. Some of us are hardcore escape artists landing up in all sorts of bother long after the game has ended. But most of us are like the child who can't wait to be found and when found can't wait to tell the whole world how perfectly hidden they were. GOD's children can't wait to be found but we do like pretending sometimes.

Thank you Lord for keeping your eye on us.

Amen

LETTERS *for* CHRISTIANS

86
GODLESS

Life without GOD. Think of an empty street on a freezing winter's night with gale force winds hammering away at the road signs as the street bends away up ahead into what lies beyond and out of sight. It's hard to comprehend what life without GOD is like but we should try because it's the fate that awaits us if we pretend everything's going to be alright. *Don't worry, be happy* is a jingle we hear a lot on the radio. They got the first part right but let's pause and think about what happiness means.

Lord, the logic of your ways confound the wicked but not your church.

Amen

EVERYDAY LOVE

87
GOD BLESS

The message of the letters in this pocketbook has been that we should encourage and love one another with the love that CHRIST had for us all. Psalm 90 is a marker of the bitter hardship experienced by Moses, one of the greatest leaders who has lived and who along with all his people struggled to please GOD. As we struggle today but for one saving grace: JESUS CHRIST, our redeemer, in whom GOD delights. But we dare not succumb to what this world offers as happiness because it's a desolate street with no end that awaits those who dabble in its vanity and pride. May THE LORD be with us all unto the end of our days when we look forward to being reunited with HIM—at peace and free of sin forever.

Lord, bless those who search for you and find you. Keep them safe from evil.

Amen

LETTERS *for* CHRISTIANS

88
ONE TO ANOTHER

If we were to write a letter to THE LORD now, what would we say? Many of us haven't tried writing a letter to HIM with pen and paper or even electronically. We've prayed—and prayer is a letter—but to write a letter with a pen seems too daunting for many of us. Or are we just too lazy! Maybe the words just don't seem to be perfect enough and we'd want to constantly edit things out in case we're saying something wrong or stupid. But if we can pray, surely we can write that prayer down. Then again, why not gift a prayer letter to someone special? It's a different way of organising our thoughts, of thinking, and of engaging with people. So, let's be brave and start writing letters, especially handwritten ones.

Lord, let's start writing to you
—by writing to one another.

Amen

EVERYDAY LOVE

89

DEAR LORD

This prayer is for discernment as we're about to read Psalm 90 again, holding the words of Moses dear to our hearts, because these are confusing times and many will be deceived. It's true LORD that today we too are being tempted into the wilderness and should expect it since YOUR WORD confirms what is to pass. But however this may come to pass, if it is by accepting the false offer of convenience in our lives, we pray for guidance and to remain standing with YOUR CHURCH. Let us not be like blind sheep milling around in confusion but grant us eyes to see.

Thank you for the lives we're able to lead. May we be useful to you in everything we do because what we do is a reflection of our faith in you. So, help us to take care in what we say and how we act. PRAISE YOUR HOLY NAME and keep us safe from the evil one. For thine is the kingdom, the power and the glory, forever and ever.

Amen

LETTERS *for* CHRISTIANS

90
PSALM 90

A prayer of Moses the man of God.

1 Lord, you have been our dwelling place
  throughout all generations.
2 Before the mountains were born
  or you brought forth the whole world,
  from everlasting to everlasting you are God.

3 You turn people back to dust,
  saying, "Return to dust, you mortals."
4 A thousand years in your sight
  are like a day that has just gone by,
  or like a watch in the night.
5 Yet you sweep people away in the sleep of death—
  they are like the new grass of the morning:
6 In the morning it springs up new,
  but by evening it is dry and withered.

7 We are consumed by your anger
  and terrified by your indignation.
8 You have set our iniquities before you,
  our secret sins in the light of your presence.
9 All our days pass away under your wrath;
  we finish our years with a moan.
10 Our days may come to seventy years,
  or eighty, if our strength endures;

EVERYDAY LOVE

    yet the best of them are but trouble and sorrow,
    for they quickly pass, and we fly away.
11 If only we knew the power of your anger!
    Your wrath is as great as the fear that is your due.
12 Teach us to number our days,
    that we may gain a heart of wisdom.

13 Relent, Lord! How long will it be?
    Have compassion on your servants.
14 Satisfy us in the morning with your unfailing love,
    that we may sing for joy and be glad all our days.
15 Make us glad for as many days as you have afflicted us,
    for as many years as we have seen trouble.
16 May your deeds be shown to your servants,
    your splendor to their children.

17 May the favor of the Lord our God rest on us;
    establish the work of our hands for us—
    yes, establish the work of our hands. (NIV)

Amen

www.ingramcontent.com/pod-product-compliance
Lightning Source LLC
Chambersburg PA
CBHW041504010526
44118CB00001B/11